101 DINOSAUR JOKES

BY PHIL HIRSCH

illustrated by Brian Boniak

SCHOLASTIC INC.
New York Toronto London Auckland Sydney

Dedicated
with a dinosaur's roar
of approval
to
TAD
from someone who knew you when.

ISBN 0-590-41691-X

Copyright © 1988 by Phil Hirsch.
All rights reserved. Published by Scholastic Inc.

12 11 10 9 8 7 6 5 4 3 2   9/8 0 1 2 3/9
Printed in the U.S.A.   01
First Scholastic printing, November 1988

101 DINOSAUR JOKES

PREHYSTERICAL LAUGHS

How do we know the age of dinosaurs?

By going to their birthday parties!

How do you dress for a dinosaur birthday party?

In a suit of armor!

How do you make a dinosaur float?

Two scoops of ice cream, some soda water, and one dinosaur!

How many dinosaurs fit into a Volkswagen?

Who knows — but sixteen Volkswagens fit into a dinosaur!

What do you do if dinosaurs invade your town?

Wake up!

What do archaeologists dig the most?

Fossils, of course!

Are reptiles good to eat?

Only if you like indigestion!

Bumper Sticker: Did you hug your dinosaur today?

What's the worst part of eating dinosaur?

You have leftovers for weeks and weeks!

Do dinosaurs have a good sense of smell?

No, or they'd smell themselves and jump off a cliff!

Oh, come on. You know dinosaurs don't smell.

They do when they miss their baths!

Why did the scientist run a red light?

Because his bumper sticker read
I ONLY BRAKE FOR DINOSAURS!

How do you make an eight-hundred-
ton dinosaur move?

With dino-mite!

Which American pioneer do dinosaurs love?

Daniel Bone!

Why don't dinosaurs take guitar lessons?

They become unstrung too easily!

Why did dinosaurs walk so slowly?

Because they didn't have jogging shoes back then!

What did dinosaurs do during the Dark Ages?

They turned on electric lights!

Where did hungry dinosaurs find cavemen?

At the Cave Inn!

FAMOUS DINOSAUR PROVERBS

A fiend in need is a fiend indeed.

His bite is worse than his bark.

Never let the left claw know what the right claw is undoing.

Here today, gone tomorrow.

Only a dinosaur can make a molehill out of a mountain.

There's no fiend like an old fiend.

It takes one to gnaw one.

You are what you eat.

CREATURE FEATURE

How do you call a dinosaur who is sixty feet long and more than fifteen feet high?

Preferably, long distance!

Do dinosaurs make good construction workers?

Well, they certainly know how to raise the roof!

Do dinosaurs really make good construction workers?

Actually, they make good destruction workers!

Do dinosaurs make good house pets?

Only if they are housebroken!

Could you feed those giant creatures potatoes?

Sure, but only with dino-sour cream!

Why did the dinosaur owner feel confident about walking his pet in the city?

He never saw a sign that said
NO DINOSAURS ALLOWED!

Why did dinosaurs become extinct?
1) They didn't brush their teeth after each meal.
2) A fatal epidemic of split ends.
3) Acid indigestion.

What comes after extinction?

Y-tinction, of course!

And what comes after Y-tinction?

Z-end!

Are dinosaurs good with cameras?

Sure, they're always snapping at something!

How long was the Age of Reptiles?

Oh, about 120 million years — give or take a year or two!

When you are 120 million years old, what do they call you?

An old fossil!

THE BEAST MOVIES IN DINOSAURLAND!

Jaws

You Are What You Eat

The Mouth That Roared

Dr. Jekyll and Mr. Dinosaur Hide

Bone Yesterday

Cast a Giant Shadow

MORE MOVIES
FOR MONSTERS

Tails of Terror

And Then There Were None

The Angry Breed

Grief Encounter

Catch 22 Cavemen

D.O.A. (Dinosaur on Arrival)

DINO-MANIA!

What is the first thing a dinosaur does if you sell it the Brooklyn Bridge?

It takes a terrible toll on you!

How much do you pay to ride a dinosaur?

Who knows — but it's un-fare!

How did the dinosaur go on a diet?

It ate a cottage-cheese factory!

If the three primary forms of rock are igneous, metamorphic, and sedimentary, which rock was not around during the Age of the Dinosaurs?

Rock and roll!

How do you take a dinosaur's temperature?

With a six-mile-long thermometer!

Are geologists music lovers?

Sure, they dig rock.

How do you know if a dinosaur is a vegetarian or a meat eater?

Lie down on a plate, silly!

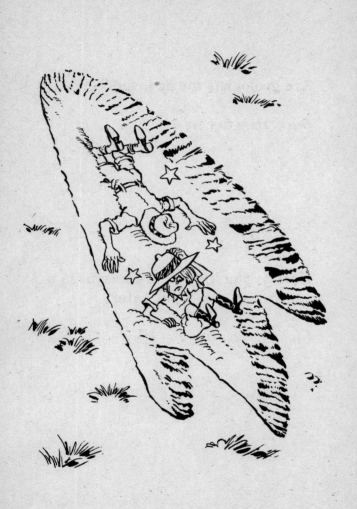

How do we know dinosaurs raced competitively?

Scientists discovered dinosaur tracks!

What was the dinosaurs' most
spectacular achievement?

*They looked so scary they didn't have
to dress up for Halloween!*

What were dinosaurs in their heyday?

An endangering species!

Why did dinosaur teeth keep falling out?

Who knows — maybe they'd have stayed in longer if fluoride toothpaste had been around!

What ear trouble did the fish-eating dinosaurs have?

They were hard of herring!

What is the difference between a dinosaur and a dragon?

Dinosaurs are too young to smoke!

Which museum dinosaur is royalty?

Bony Prince Charlie!

Are you sure Bony Prince Charlie is royalty?

Well, he married Lady Di-nosaur, didn't he?

Which illness was common among the brontosaurus?

Dino-sore throats!

What did the dinosaur eat?

Anything it wanted!

Why don't we see any flying
dinosaurs today?

*No air traffic controller would clear
one for landing.*

THE DINOSAUR INTELLIGENCE TEST

(Please do not take this test unless you are a registered dinosaur.)

Question #1:
How would a dinosaur come in handy today?
1) It would make a great watchdog.
2) Riding a dinosaur would impress people on a horseback riding trail.
3) On a leash it would make a terrific conversation piece.
4) None of the above.

Question #2:
Where do you find dinosaurs?
1) The same place you left them.
2) In dino-saw mills.
3) In a dream — a *bite*mare.

Question #3:
Why did some dinosaurs have very
long necks?
1) So they could wear *big* turtleneck
   sweaters.
2) So they could bird-watch.
3) Because they were liars, and
   every time they told a fib, their
   necks grew!
4) They liked to wear necklaces — a
   hundred of them.

Question #4:
What do you say when a ferocious
dinosaur knocks at your door?
1) "We gave at the office."
2) "There's an epidemic of bubonic
plague in the house, so I can't
let you in."
3) "The next-door neighbor tastes
better."
4) "Nobody's home."

Question #5:
Who taught some of these reptiles
to fly?
1) The Wrong Brothers.
2) Nobody — they just winged it.
3) An astro-nut.

Question #6:

If the dinosaurs disappeared about seventy million years ago, where did they go?
   1) A UFO came along and took them to another planet.
   2) They haven't disappeared — they're just hiding.
   3) A movie director has frozen them all — and is ready to thaw them for his scariest movie!

Answers:
1. 5; **2.** 4; **3.** 5; **4.** 5; **5.** 4; **6.** 4.

Note:
If you've answered all the questions correctly, you win a free dinosaur ride — if you can find a dinosaur!

FUNNY
BUT FEROCIOUS

Did the cavemen have trouble stuffing
a dinosaur for Thanksgiving?

*No. Forty cavemen were enough to
stuff one dinosaur — unless it was
extra hungry!*

Did the dinosaur know anything
about division?

Well, it could easily bite you in two!

Did cavemen and cavewomen wear dinosaur teeth as necklaces?

Sure, anytime a dinosaur bit one of them in the neck!

What did the dinosaur say when it saw the volcano erupt?

"Lava-ly day, isn't it?"

What did they say about the famous dinosaur singer?

She was dino-mite!

What were the great dinosaur
hunter's first words?

Goo-goo, ga-ga!

Did the dinosaurs have a labor union?

*Who knows — but they certainly knew
how to strike!*

What did the sign say when a dinosaur union member picketed?

"More prey for less work!"

How did young dinosaurs get an increase in allowance?

By putting the bite on their parents!

Why do geologists admire dinosaurs?

Because geologists have rocks in their heads!

What do you get if a dinosaur tries to use you for a punching bag?

Claws-trophobia!

What did the iguana say when it met the dinosaur?

IGUANA GO HOME!

DINOSAUR OLDIES BUT GOODIES
(jokes with some bite in them)

This dinosaur booked passage on a cruise ship and was seen entering one of the dining rooms shortly after the liner set sail.

"Would you care for a menu?" asked the maître d'.

"No thanks," said the dinosaur. "Just bring me everyone on the passenger list."

Did you hear about the dinosaur who went into the flea circus and ended up stealing the whole show?

Did you hear about the crazy, mixed-up dinosaur who ate only libraries?

It wanted to be well fed and well read!

A museum curator rushed frantically to the nearest telephone. Standing nearby was a dinosaur with a piece of the curator's pants hanging from its mouth.

"Operator! Operator!" screamed the panic-stricken curator. "Connect me with the nearest taxidermist. I want to report some unfinished business."

Exactly how old are dinosaurs?

*Who knows — but on their birthdays,
I'd like to be selling candles!*

THOSE SILLY DINOSAURS!

Do dinosaurs make good waiters?

Yes, because they can sure dish it out!

What do you know if you find a dinosaur in your soup?

That you'll be the next course!

Could you have made a pet of a
dinosaur?

Only if you had a thirty-mile leash!

Why don't dinosaurs go to Burger King?

They can have it their way no matter where they eat!

Who said "All's well that ends well"?

Everyone — when the dinosaurs became extinct!

If you had fourteen dinosaurs in your bedroom, what would you have?
1) An extremely large bedroom.
2) Room for improvement.
3) No worry about robbers breaking in.
4) All of the above.

What did the dinosaurs do when the Ice Age came?

What else — they went skating!

Do dinosaurs have trouble mailing letters?

No, they always have plenty of stamps!

How do you know when a dinosaur likes you?

It gives you a stamp of approval!

Do archaeologists have plenty of help digging up dinosaur bones?

No, they usually work with a skeleton crew.

When was the worst time to be a doctor?

When a dinosaur patient had a sore throat!

Why were dinosaurs the enemies of cavemen?

Because dinosaurs caused cave-ins!

When did the dinosaur get out its golf clubs?

The day it saw the Grand Canyon!

How did the lost continent of Atlantis disappear?

Three heavy dinosaurs stepped on it.

What happens if you cross a dinosaur with a parrot?

Nobody's sure. But if it spoke, everybody would listen!

What did the clown do when he saw the dinosaur head mounted on the wall?

He went into the next room to see the rest of it!

How did some of the dinosaurs learn to fly?

Simple. Dino-see, dino-soar!

Why did some dinosaurs choose to live in the water and some on land?

It was either slink or swim!

What's the best way to measure a dinosaur?

With a forty-thousand-inch ruler!

MOTTOS FOR DINOS

Beauty is only skin deep — but ugly is to the bone!

Dinosaurs are not covered by a warranty!

Dinosaurs don't believe in survival of the fittest.

Dinosaurs like to throw their weight around.

Bone up on some old fossils.

Adopt a dinosaur — help feed a starving creature.

Museum dinosaurs look bone tired.

DID YOU HUG YOUR DINOSAUR TODAY?

MONSTER-OUS JOKES!

How fast must you run if a dinosaur is chasing you?

One step faster than the dinosaur!

Which were the helmeted dinosaurs?

The ones who rode motorcycles!

How do dinosaurs decide when to take a bite?

They use snap *judgment!*

When did the tyrannosaurus rex use Band-Aids?

Anytime they had dino-sores!

What can you say about the eubrontes, a three-toed dinosaur?

It was two toe much!

Can the eubrontes think on its feet?

That's toe much to ask!

Why did the eubrontes need three toes?

So it could count past one plus one!

What did the other dinosaurs think about the eubrontes?

They thought the eubrontes was toe-riffic!

What is the perfect spot for a
dinosaur's vacation?

No-man's land!

Why did other dinosaurs stay away
from the duck-billed dinosaur?

It had a fowl mouth!

Is there a theory that some dinosaurs
had feathers?

Yes, but it's for the birds!

What's better than a dinosaur in your bathtub?

A rubber ducky!

What's worse than a dinosaur in your bathtub?

Two dinosaurs in your bathtub!

How did dinosaurs get leaves off
branches beyond their reach?

They must have used dino-saws!

A DINOSAUR'S FAVORITE TV SHOWS

Boneanza

M*A*S*H*E*R*S

Edge of Nightmare

That's Inedible

In Search of Fossils

LAST LAUGHS

Why do the Scotch love to see
dinosaur skeletons?

They think they're bonny and bony!

Were dinosaurs good sports?

No, they were dino-sore losers!

Would a dinosaur like modern life?

No, because it couldn't fit into a compact car!

What do dinosaurs have that no other animals have?

Little dinosaurs!

Did dinosaurs know how to use the telephone?

Probably — after all, the croco-dials!

Did some dinosaurs have horns?

Only those that were musically inclined!

Which dinosaurs loved to eat?

The diner-saurs!

Which dinosaurs slept twenty hours a day?

The dino-snores!